Building Resiliency

How to Thrive in Times of Change

IDEAS INTO ACTION GUIDEBOOKS

Aimed at managers and executives who are concerned with their own and others' development, each guidebook in this series gives specific advice on how to complete a developmental task or solve a leadership problem.

LEAD CONTRIBUTORS	Mary Lynn Pulley
	Michael Wakefield
CONTRIBUTOR	Ellen Van Velsor
GUIDEBOOK ADVISORY GROUP	Victoria A. Guthrie
	Cynthia D. McCauley
	Russ S. Moxley
DIRECTOR OF ASSESSMENTS, TOOLS, AND PUBLICATIONS	Sylvester Taylor
MANAGER, PUBLICATION DEVELOPMENT	Peter Scisco
WRITER	Rebecca Garau
DESIGN AND LAYOUT	Joanne Ferguson
CONTRIBUTING ARTISTS	Laura J. Gibson
	Chris Wilson, 29 & Company

CCL No. 413
ISBN-13: 978-1-882197-67-5
ISBN-10: 1-882197-67-4

CENTER FOR CREATIVE LEADERSHIP
WWW.CCL.ORG

AN IDEAS INTO ACTION GUIDEBOOK

Building Resiliency

How to Thrive in Times of Change

Mary Lynn Pulley and Michael Wakefield

Center for
Creative
Leadership®

THE IDEAS INTO ACTION GUIDEBOOK SERIES

This series of guidebooks draws on the practical knowledge that the Center for Creative Leadership (CCL®) has generated in the course of more than thirty years of research and educational activity conducted in partnership with hundreds of thousands of managers and executives. Much of this knowledge is shared – in a way that is distinct from the typical university department, professional association, or consultancy. CCL is not simply a collection of individual experts, although the individual credentials of its staff are impressive; rather it is a community, with its members holding certain principles in common and working together to understand and generate practical responses to today's leadership and organizational challenges.

The purpose of the series is to provide managers with specific advice on how to complete a developmental task or solve a leadership challenge. In doing that, the series carries out CCL's mission to advance the understanding, practice, and development of leadership for the benefit of society worldwide. We think you will find the Ideas Into Action Guidebooks an important addition to your leadership toolkit.

Table of Contents

EXECUTIVE BRIEF

It may be human nature to resist change – particularly when it's delivered as a hardship, disappointment, or rejection. But by developing resiliency managers can not only survive change, but learn, grow, and thrive in it. In fact, for leaders, developing resiliency is critical. Resiliency helps managers deal with the pressures and uncertainties of being in charge in organizations today.

This guidebook defines resiliency, explains why it's important, and describes how you can develop your own store of resiliency. It focuses on nine developmental components that, taken together, create a sense of resiliency and increase your ability to handle the unknown and to view change – whether from disappointment or success – as an opportunity for development.

What Is Resiliency?

Resiliency provides the ability to recover quickly from change, hardship, or misfortune. It's associated with elasticity, buoyancy, and adaptation. Resilient people demonstrate flexibility, durability, an attitude of optimism, and openness to learning. A lack of resilience is signaled by burnout, fatigue, malaise, depression, defensiveness, and cynicism.

Resiliency is the product of a broad perspective. You can bolster it with a supportive network of professional and personal relationships, and use it to become comfortable with change. Resiliency taps into your ability to adapt even as it relies on your own knowledge about yourself – your values, confidence, and optimism. And it's a key element to success on all levels and in all aspects of your life, from professional career development and leadership opportunities to the pursuit of personal goals and well-being.

People often have the view that resiliency means being unflappable, strong, or unaffected. Most of us have heard the saying, "When the going gets tough, the tough get going." But resiliency isn't simply a matter of "toughing it out." Bearing up under pressure is certainly part of being resilient, but just one part. Marathon runners, for example, have to be tough to endure a grueling 26-mile run, and yet it's often their ability to handle the intangibles (weather, unknown competition, attitude about ability, a slight but nagging injury at the 20-mile marker) that puts them across the finish line and in the winner's circle.

Developing resiliency requires that you pay attention to the complexities of your experiences, listen to your emotions, and be willing to learn from disappointment as well as success.

A Tale of Resilience

Straight out of college, Matt began working for a national grocery chain. For 16 years, he did very well. Shortly after accepting a significant promotion, things began to change. Struggles with his new supervisor overshadowed his work for the next two years, whittling away at his confidence and job satisfaction. Eventually, his job was eliminated and he was laid off.

Matt did not rush immediately into a rigorous job search. "I did a lot of self-evaluation in terms of where I was and how marketable I was … I tried to step back and not rush into anything," he says. He spent more time with his family and began getting involved in the community and with his church.

After a three-month break, Matt felt rejuvenated and began a diligent, focused process of networking and job searching. Through a series of contacts, he was offered a job in a related field. Over time, Matt began to see how much he learned from the loss of his job. On the work front, he realized he needed to do a better job of "managing up" – communicating with his boss and his boss's boss. Personally, he learned that maintaining a more balanced life is an effective long-term way to cope with life's ups and downs. After two years on the new job, he had grown his region's business by 20 percent, while at the same time continuing his focus on family and community.

Matt believes losing his job was a blessing in disguise: "It was not a catastrophic event. There was a paradigm shift, but it wasn't a catastrophe."

Why Is Resiliency Important?

In 1984 CCL conducted a study on the "key events" that contributed to leaders' development. Twenty percent of respondents said they learned significant lessons from hardships, such as a job loss, career setbacks, mistakes and failures, or personal trauma. The research was repeated in the late 1990s. At that time 34 percent of respondents cited hardships as key learning experiences. That 14 percent increase reflects an increasing complexity and turbulence – and it underscores the importance of developing resiliency.

Resiliency is important because change is so pervasive. Think for a moment about the kinds of changes today's organization typically encounters and how they might affect your leadership skills, your managerial performance, even your career. Organizations can change mission, strategy, or global focus. Outside and inside business environments, as well as markets, can shift.

How does a manager flourish, even survive, in a current of constant and complex change? By building skills in resiliency, by broadening perspectives and competencies so that organizational, personal, and career changes can be absorbed and contribute to your leadership development.

Becoming Resilient

Beginning early in life you have developed behaviors and perspectives that have enhanced or hindered your ability to be resilient and adaptable as an adult. Yet resiliency can be developed. It's possible to change your views, habits, and responses by modifying your thoughts and actions in nine areas: acceptance of change, continuous learning, self empowerment, sense of purpose, personal identity, personal and professional networks, reflection, skill shifting, and your relationship to money.

9

These nine areas aren't separate facets of resilience but intertwined and interrelated themes. Each builds on the others, influences the others, and in concert with the others can bolster your resiliency and your skill in handling change. By improving in all of these areas you broaden your outlook and become less narrowly focused – more able to adapt to change.

Acceptance of Change

Change is constant and inevitable, and to some managers it brings an overwhelming discomfort. The roots of that discomfort can sometimes be traced to such feelings as fear (*How can I continue to succeed when the rules have changed?*) or a need to exert control (*If I don't do it my way, the way I have always done it, then it won't be done right*). Other managers try to deny change by focusing on the skills that have brought them past success and ignoring gaps in their leadership competencies. But sooner or later a change for which they are not prepared results in a mistake with serious consequences – a missed promotion, negative appraisal, demotion, or termination.

> *"He couldn't change. He had a rigid and outdated management style. He was inflexible and people got tired of it."*

Successful managers accept change and adapt to it. If you find yourself uncomfortable with the idea of change, you can increase your resiliency in this area by creating an accurate portrait of yourself and an accurate picture of your environment. Here are three actions you can take to build up your resiliency by becoming more accepting of and adaptable to change.

1. Pay attention to the people and the work around you. Don't bury yourself in a narrow channel of work or you risk being blindsided. Seek out new challenges that stretch your skills or that minimize your weaknesses.
2. Pay attention to your physical and mental well-being. If you feel discomfort, which is natural when changes occur,

take that as a signal to further explore your feelings and thoughts about the change. Use the Resiliency Worksheet on pages 22 and 23 as a guide to exploring your reaction to change.

3. Examine change on its own terms. Decide which changes you can control and which changes you can't control. For example, if your organization gives your team a new performance mandate, you manage that change through your team leadership. But if your organization undergoes a downsizing or reacts dramatically to a market shift, that kind of change is beyond what you can control. In that case it's better to move your energies away from the anxiety spawned by the change and toward developing new skills and bolstering current strengths.

> **Accepting Change Is Crucial**
>
> According to research from the Center for Creative Leadership (CCL), the number one reason managers derail – fall off the "track of success" – is their inability to change or adapt during a transition. North American managers said 55 percent of the most successful managers they knew displayed the ability to adapt (European managers put the number even higher at 67 percent). That ability to adapt, that resiliency, was the most frequently mentioned success factor in CCL's most recent study of executive derailment.

Continuous Learning

The nature of resiliency asks that you acquire new skills and understanding and be able to apply them during times of change. Many managers resist learning new ways, holding on to old behaviors and skills even when changes make it obvious that they don't work anymore. If you find yourself in that description, think about your resistance. It may be that you think your old ways are important to who you are and that changing might somehow affect your identity. Your old skills and behaviors might be deeply connected to your self-worth, your self-esteem; they might make you feel valuable when unfamiliar skills don't. You may cling to your old habits because you don't want to feel less competent during that clumsy learning stage when you take on new skills.

"Take as much time as you can learning so that you don't use your own experiences when they really don't apply."

To get started on a path to continuous learning, and to overcome any resistance you might feel, try these techniques:

- At the end of each day write down one thing you learned or one thing you knew already but had confirmed.
- Review a professional disappointment that occurred early in your career or at least six months ago (far enough in the past for you to have gained some perspective on the experience). What do you know now that you didn't know then? What did you learn from that experience? What knowledge was confirmed by that experience? What knowledge was proved wrong?
- Look back on a professional success that occurred early in your career or at least six months ago. What do you know now that you didn't know then? What did you learn from that experience? What knowledge was confirmed by that experience? What knowledge was proved wrong?

12

The Learning Curve Is Upside Down

The "learning curve" is usually depicted as a gradual incline, illustrating that as you learn, your performance improves. In  reality, learning almost always causes a drop in performance before improvements come about. This completely natural process can cause discomfort for managers hoping to develop new stores of resiliency by adding to their interpersonal and technical skills. The  learning curve is not a gradual rise in performance but is a drop in performance followed by improvement.

Self Empowerment

Your power to build resiliency lies within you. Accessing it is a matter of choice. In an era of downsizing, restructuring, market shifts, and technological change it's important that you take charge of your own career and your own self-development. The implied employment contract (work hard for an organization and be rewarded lifetime employment and perhaps a steady rise in responsibility) has given way to free agency. Don't expect someone else to guide your career. Approach your work with an entrepreneurial spirit. Create

"The organization needed an area supervisor in one of its departments. My boss sent me to take on the responsibility even though I'd never had that kind of position before. He said that he knew I wasn't trained and that I had never done this, but he was sure that I could do it and to just do what I had to do to get the job done. I found out soon enough I could handle a group position. It improved my confidence in myself."

13

resiliency by giving yourself the freedom to make your own choices and to act on them.

Here are a few ideas that can help steer you toward a more resilient attitude toward your place in the world of work.

- Identify the strengths you have that you can rely on or turn to. Try this exercise: List your strengths, and then ask yourself: *Where else can I fit in this organization?* What other positions are there – either real or imagined – in which you can ply your strengths in a different environment?
- Develop new strengths by taking on "stretch" assignments. Look outside of work for developmental opportunities and find safe ways to practice new skills. For example, you could practice becoming a better team leader by volunteering to lead a committee at your child's school, by serving on a community arts council, or through some other volunteer assignment.
- Create your own "board of directors." Ideally this is a group of your peers – highly trusted – from outside your organization but who have roughly the same level of responsibility as you. Meet on a regular basis to discuss common challenges and solutions.

Sense of Purpose

Develop a "personal why" that gives your work meaning or helps you put it into a larger context. A clear sense of purpose helps you to see setbacks from a broader perspective.

Have you ever been "in the flow"? When you are engrossed in something you care deeply about, time slips by and at the end of the process you feel energized, not drained. Think back on

> *"I believe that I got through these challenges for a purpose, and the purpose is that sometime down the road I'm going to have to help somebody, and if I hadn't experienced them [challenges], how could I do that with any credibility?"*

Reveal Your Sense of Purpose

Sit down with these questions designed to unearth and bolster your sense of purpose. After reading each question, take some time to write out a response. As a follow-up to this activity, sit down with a trusted friend who can ask you these same questions. Answer as fully as you can. When you are finished, your friend begins again with the first question. Repeat the series of questions several times. If your friend is also interested in rediscovering a sense of purpose, you can take turns asking and answering the questions.

1. What is the ideal to which you are striving? What is your preferred future?
2. What is your current state? Where are you now in relation to where you want to be?
3. What does remaining in your current state get you? What does your current state do for you?
4. What have you used your current state for? What have you used it to justify?
5. What have you used your current state to avoid?
6. What would you face if you were not at your current state?
7. What have you used your current state to be, to have, or to do?
8. What have you used your current state to not be, to not have, or to not do?
9. What is blocking you from moving away from your current state?
10. What are you going to do about changing your current state?

your encounters with that kind of experience. Those encounters are likely tied closely to the goals most important to you. Here are a few questions that can help you explore your sense of purpose:

- What is your most important value? What do you do at work or away from the job that reflects that value?
- What was one of your childhood dreams? Identify the crossroads in your life that led you away from that dream. Why did you take those different paths?
- If there were no obstacles (financial, personal, or other), what would you like to do with your life?
- Review your answer to the previous question. What's the first step you could take toward meeting that goal?

Personal Identity

Your job is just one facet of your identity, and your career is just one aspect of your life. To achieve some degree of resilience you have to separate who you are from what you do. It's a long-term developmental process, but worth the effort. That separation will keep you resilient during times of career disappointments or personal hardship by giving you the freedom to focus on your strengths and opportunity rather than your anxiety and loss. The attributes of your personal identity create an authenticity that stands with you throughout times of change and creates alignment between your feelings, beliefs, values, and actions. Authenticity creates a platform for resiliency. Here are a few ideas to try and some questions to think about if you want to strengthen your sense of personal identity:

> *"I came to the realization of who I was, and that there's a difference between who I am and what I do."*

- Develop a personal logo. You can design it yourself or modify an existing design. Think about what a personal logo might mean, how it can stand for what you are just as a company logo represents the values and mission of an organization.
- Develop a personal metaphor for your goals. Think about where you are right now and write down three facts about

16

yourself. Now write down three feelings evoked by those facts. Finally, complete this sentence with those feelings in mind: "This feels like . . . ." To create a future-directed metaphor, think about where you would like to be or what you would like to accomplish during the next year (or choose your own time frame) and repeat this three-point exercise. Examine your "future metaphor" and try to observe and catch yourself behaving that way in your daily activities.

- List all the different roles you play in your professional life. List all the roles you would like to play in your professional life. What changes would you have to make to close that gap and to get closer to the roles you want to play?

- List some early "childhood commandments" (*You need something practical to fall back on. If you want something done right you have to do it yourself.*) What part did they play in creating the sense of identity you have now? How do they block you from the personal identity you imagine for yourself?

Personal and Professional Networks

Resilient managers cultivate a broad network of personal and professional relationships. They are less reliant on a single organization and use personal relationships to create a strong base of support – a critical element in achieving goals, dealing with hardships, and developing perspective.

But personal and professional networks aren't just safety nets you use to break your fall in times of trouble. They are a series of mutually

"If you have developed a good-sized network, you can duplicate that network anywhere you go. That is truly a transferable skill. And the network where you are will still be there. It's not like, I sold my house and it's not mine anymore. I can pick up the phone with people I haven't talked with in four or five years. A network endures."

giving and receiving connections through which you collaborate, share perspectives, broaden your worldview, strengthen your vision, teach and learn new skills, and stay attuned to your environment. The key to building networks that add to your resiliency is to make the connections personal. Try this simple four-step exercise to build, or to reevaluate, your personal and professional networks:

1. Make a list of the people you can depend on in times of need.
2. Add to that list the people with whom you would first share stories of success.
3. How much do you know about each of the people on this list?
4. Choose a name from the list – what can you do for that person today?

Another tactic you can use to identify people for your personal network is to choose someone you admire at work. Identify that person's strengths and watch how he or she handles different situations – especially those related to changes in the organization or the environment. What kinds of positive behaviors do they exhibit? How could you emulate that behavior in your current position?

Reflection

The demands of meeting business objectives can make it difficult to find time for reflection, even during good times. That difficulty intensifies during times of stress, such as when an organization downsizes, when a career is threatened with derailment, or when a personal crisis demands intense emotional attention. Even so, it's important

"My job is to increase sales by 5 percent each and every year. Reflection is nice and all that, but the bottom line is if it doesn't increase sales, it's not my job. If I was a poet, maybe I'd reflect more – but I'm not."

18

How to Keep a Reflection Journal

Keeping a journal is an effective tool for building resiliency by creating deeper self-awareness. CCL recommends the use of a personal learning journal as a way to gain the insight necessary to become more adaptable. The form and content of your journal is a matter of individual choice. However, there are typically three parts to a journal entry:

1. *Event or experience.* Describe what occurred as objectively as possible. Don't use judgmental language. Stick to the facts. What happened? Who was involved? When did it happen? Where did it happen?

2. *Reaction.* Describe your reaction to the event as factually and objectively as possible. What did you want to do in response to the event? What did you actually do? What were your thoughts? What were your feelings?

3. *Lessons.* Think about the experience and your reaction to it. What did you learn from the event and from your reaction to it? Did the event suggest a developmental challenge you should address? Do you see a pattern in your reactions? Did you react differently than in the past during similar experiences and does that suggest you are making progress or backsliding on a valuable leadership competency?

to make time for reflection whether you're riding a success or enduring a hardship.

By taking time to reflect you can develop a degree of self-awareness that can enhance your resiliency in handling your professional and personal world. Think of reflection as an effective self-feedback tool. You may find yourself resisting change or being unable to accept change because by censoring yourself you aren't open to this valuable feedback channel. If you find reflection diffi-cult to work into your day, here are some suggestions:

- establish structures or routines that build in reflection
- rearrange priorities to make time for reflection
- use performance appraisal information as occasion for re-flection
- keep a journal.

Skill Shifting

Don't be afraid to question and even change your definition of yourself or your career. Reframe how you see your skills in relation to your organiza-tion, to your values, and to your goals. By casting your talents in a new light you can see how your skills might shift into new patterns of work and behavior.

To help you gain new perspective on familiar skills, try these suggestions:

"Our current leader leads by example without publicity. This person has overcome great handicaps to reach the highest ranks in society coming from the lowest social strata. Now he gives back to our local communities. His positive example of consistent service means a great deal to our organization."

- Identify the skills that you have and that you use in the work-place, at home, and in your com-munity. Where else might these skills play out? Experiment with volunteer activities to try out different behaviors and to stretch your technical skills into unfamiliar territory without the pressure of job performance.
- Describe five different jobs / careers that you could do today given your current skills.

Relationship to Money

Building resiliency isn't always about enhancing your interpersonal and technical skills or recasting your talents in new ways. Resiliency also comes from reviewing how you relate to the outside world. Perhaps this is nowhere more evident than when it comes to your attitude toward money. Living beyond or even to the very limit of your means limits your flexibility in the face of change.

> *"I know I can always get income from somewhere – maybe five or six places, but income will come in. That's not the most important thing."*

Here is a short exercise that can help you reorient your relationship to money.

1. Look at your personal budget. List the things you need and the things you want.

2. Examine your budget to determine the minimum amount of income you need to cover necessities. Think of and describe alternative ways to earn that income.

3. If there's a gap between what you want and the money that's available, prioritize your want list.

4. What are some alternative ways to earn money to get the things you want? What are some of the things on your want list that can wait?

5. If money were not an obstacle, which of the things on your want list would you still want? Rank your choices.

6. If time were not an obstacle, which of the things on your want list would you still want? Rank your choices.

Resiliency Worksheet

Look over the items in this checklist and darken the circle that most closely matches your assessment of yourself in each of the nine resiliency areas. What does your list tell you about your degree of resiliency? What resiliency strengths can you rely on during times of change? What areas should you develop to become more resilient?

Resiliency Strength	Resiliency Development Need
(indicates a skill you can rely on in times of change)	*(indicates a skill you should develop to increase your resiliency)*

Acceptance of Change

I am comfortable with change. I see it as an opportunity to grow as a leader.	Change makes me uneasy. I don't like facing new challenges without having some kind of control over the situation.

O   O   O   O   O   O   O

Continuous Learning

Change provides a chance for me to learn new skills and test new ideas. I like to build on the lessons of the past – my successes and my disappointments.	I want to stick with what I know best and with the skills that got me to this point in my career. Other people expect that – it's part of who I am.

O   O   O   O   O   O   O

Self Empowerment

I regularly assess my strengths. I keep my eye out for work assignments that will let me build new managerial skills and develop as a leader.	I have enough on my hands guiding the work of my direct reports. If this organization wants me to develop, it has to give me some kind of plan.

O   O   O   O   O   O   O

Sense of Purpose

I like to think that my work reflects my personal values. I try to make decisions based on what's important to me and balance that with the organization's mission.	If the organization demands a certain way of working, who am I to say if it's right? My work isn't designed to follow a value system. It's my life the way it is – I can't just change it around to make it into something else.

O   O   O   O   O   O   O

Personal Identity

I really like my job, but it doesn't define who I am. I have other pursuits outside of work that are just as important to me as my job.

I live for my work. Why not? What's the first question a person usually asks you? It's "What do you do?" not "How would you describe yourself?"

O   O   O   O   O   O   O

Personal and Professional Networks

I really appreciate my family, my friends, and my colleagues. There have been many times that those relationships have helped me out of a jam. I like to stay connected to those people who are close to me and take a personal interest in their lives.

Networking is really helpful in case there's a downturn and my company downsizes me. I wish I could stay more current with what my friends and colleagues are doing outside of work, but there never seems to be enough time.

O   O   O   O   O   O   O

Reflection

I make some room in each day to reflect on my decisions and actions. I like to look back to see if there was another choice I could have made.

There are always so many things to do. It's like running ahead of an avalanche. I don't have time to sit back and daydream about where I am going and how I am getting there.

O   O   O   O   O   O   O

Skill Shifting

My skills could prove useful to this organization in another role. I can translate my experiences outside of work into developmental opportunities.

Every position calls for a distinct set of skills. It takes a long time to develop those skills. It's inefficient to take somebody out of a familiar role and ask them to perform some other function.

O   O   O   O   O   O   O

Relationship to Money

I like things. Doesn't everybody? But I don't want to get caught in the trap of working long hours and taking on extra assignments in order to pay for things that don't really reflect my interests and values. I make my money work for me. I think about my purchases before I make them.

I have responsibilities. They cost money. There's no way around that. Besides, there's a certain expectation that when you reach my position you can afford a certain kind of lifestyle. You just have to work hard if you want the good things in life.

O   O   O   O   O   O   O

Suggested Readings

Bridges, W. (1980). *Transitions: Making sense of life's changes.* New York: Addison-Wesley.

Bunker, K. The power of vulnerability in contemporary leadership. *Consulting Psychology Journal: Practice and Research, 49*(2), 122–136.

Lombardo, M. M., & Eichinger, R. W. (1989). *Eighty-eight assignments for development in place.* Greensboro, NC: Center for Creative Leadership.

McCauley, C. D., Moxley, R. S., & Van Velsor, E. (Eds.). (1998). *The Center for Creative Leadership handbook of leadership development.* San Francisco: Jossey-Bass.

McCall, M. W., Jr., Lombardo, M. M., & Morrison, A. M. (1988). *The lessons of experience.* Lexington, MA: Lexington Books.

Noer, D. (1993). *Healing the wounds: Overcoming the trauma of layoffs and revitalizing downsized organizations.* San Francisco: Jossey-Bass.

O'Neil, J. (1993). *The paradox of success: When winning at work means losing at life.* New York: Putnam.

Pulley, M. L. (1997). *Losing your job — reclaiming your soul: Stories of resilience, renewal, and hope.* San Francisco: Jossey-Bass.

Background

This guidebook integrates and articulates key principles taught in CCL's leadership development programs. CCL's approach to leadership development has always emphasized self-awareness and learning, critical components to building resiliency.

That emphasis is based at least partly on long-standing research CCL has conducted in the key events of executives' lives and the lessons they have learned from those experiences. CCL's examination of this area focused on three broad themes: job assignments, hardships, and formal training. In each of those areas executives made developmental strides by being resilient to the challenges provided by their experiences.

Another link to resiliency can be found in CCL's research into executive derailment that shows that resistance to change (which could contribute to a lack of resiliency) is a derailment factor and that openness to change (which could contribute to a greater degree of resiliency) leads to career and managerial success. In fact, the most frequently mentioned success factor in CCL's derailment research is the ability to develop or adapt. That ability is a key component to accepting change, which lies at the heart of the successful and resilient manager and leader.

Along with that research and coupled with CCL's educational initiatives, this guidebook draws on Mary Lynn Pulley's examination of resiliency among executives and others who survived and even thrived during professional disappointments and personal hardships. Her insight into how those survivors turned setbacks into opportunity is detailed in her 1997 book, *Losing Your Job — Reclaiming Your Soul: Stories of Resilience, Renewal, and Hope.*

Key Point Summary

Resiliency allows you to recover quickly from change, hardship, or misfortune. Resilient people demonstrate flexibility, durability, an attitude of optimism, and openness to learning. A lack of resilience is signaled by burnout, fatigue, malaise, depression, defensiveness, and cynicism. Resiliency not only gives you the tools to handle hardship and disappointment, but it allows you to develop new skills and perspectives that lead to continued success at work and away from the job.

People often view resilient people as characteristically unflappable, strong, or unaffected. But being resilient isn't the same as being tough, even though dogged determination – especially the determination to learn from mistakes and successes – plays a key role. A resilient person gets that way by broadening his or her perspective, by being open to change, and by being willing to learn.

Resiliency is important because change is so pervasive. Today's organization typically encounters all kinds of change that can affect your leadership skills, your managerial performance, even your career. It can change its mission, its global focus, or its strategy. Changes can occur to the environment in which an organization works or to the marketplace it serves. You can survive and even flourish during such times of constant and complex change by building skills in resiliency.

Resiliency can be developed. It's possible to change your views, habits, and responses by modifying your thoughts and actions in nine areas: acceptance of change, continuous learning, self empowerment, sense of purpose, personal identity, personal and professional networks, reflection, skill shifting, and your relationship to money. By becoming resilient you can absorb and learn from personal and career changes, making them key components of your leadership development.

Ordering Information

TO GET MORE INFORMATION, TO ORDER OTHER IDEAS INTO ACTION GUIDEBOOKS, OR TO FIND OUT ABOUT BULK-ORDER DISCOUNTS, PLEASE CONTACT US BY PHONE AT 336-545-2810 OR VISIT OUR ONLINE BOOKSTORE AT WWW.CCL.ORG/GUIDEBOOKS.

Other Related Publications

CRISIS LEADERSHIP: USING MILITARY LESSONS, ORGANIZATIONAL EXPERIENCES, AND THE POWER OF INFLUENCE TO LESSEN THE IMPACT OF CHAOS ON THE PEOPLE YOU LEAD

Nothing tests a leader like a crisis. The dramatic events surrounding a crisis profoundly affect the people in an organization and can even threaten the organization's survival. But there are actions a leader can take before, during, and after a crisis to effectively reduce the duration and impact of these difficult situations. Effective crisis leadership is comprised of three things – communication, clarity of vision and values, and caring relationships. Leaders who develop, pay attention to, and practice these qualities go a long way toward handling the human dimension of a crisis. (CCL Stock No. 185)

LEARNING FROM LIFE: TURNING LIFE'S LESSONS INTO LEADERSHIP EXPERIENCE

If you were to ask managers and executives where they get the most influential and effective developmental training, the answer you're likely to get is "on the job." Too often, those same managers and executives discount what can be learned from experiences outside of work. CCL research demonstrates that activities that take place outside of the workday contribute to a leader's effectiveness as a manager. This book shows how to see those activities as opportunities for developing leadership skills in such areas as interpersonal relations, communication, collaboration, and flexibility. (CCL Stock No. 407)

MAKING CREATIVITY PRACTICAL: INNOVATION THAT GETS RESULTS

The process of practical creativity provides leaders with an especially nimble problem-solving approach. The goal of the process is to produce high-quality ideas that are appropriate to the task – which means groups and organizations can implement them with less risk. (CCL Stock No. 421)

CPSIA information can be obtained
at www.ICGtesting.com
Printed in the USA
BVHW051937090120
568898BV00002B/9/P